Claw And Orde
Establishing Your Cat's R

Chapter 1: The Feline Soc

The Alpha Cat: Who's Really in Charge?

Have you ever wondered who truly runs the show in your household? Is it you, the cat owner, or is it actually your feline friend? In this subchapter, we will delve into the complex world of cat social hierarchy and determine once and for all: who's really in charge - the alpha cat!

Claw And Order
Establishing Your Cat's Rank at Home

Chapter 1: The Feline Social Structure

As cat owners, we like to think we are the ones calling the shots. We provide the food, the shelter, and the love, so obviously, we must be in charge, right? Wrong! Cats have a way of asserting their dominance and making sure we know who is really in control. From knocking things off shelves to demanding attention at all hours of the night, our feline friends have a way of keeping us on our toes.

The alpha cat in your household is the one who dictates the rules, sets the schedule, and demands the most attention. You may think you are the one making the decisions, but just watch as your cat gives you that look that says, "I'm in charge here." Whether it's deciding when it's time to be fed or when it's time for cuddles, the alpha cat always has the final say.

Claw And Order
Establishing Your Cat's Rank at Home

Chapter 1: The Feline Social Structure

But don't worry, being the alpha cat is not all fun and games. With great power comes great responsibility, and your feline friend takes their role very seriously. They may demand the best spot on the couch or the warmest spot in bed, but at the end of the day, they are just looking out for their own well-being and comfort.

So, the next time you find yourself wondering who's really in charge, just take a look at your cat's confident strut and know that the alpha cat reigns supreme in your household. Embrace your feline overlord and bask in the glory of being ruled by the most majestic creature in the animal kingdom - your beloved cat!

Claw And Order
Establishing Your Cat's Rank at Home

Chapter 1: The Feline Social Structure

The Beta Cats: The Right-Hand Cats

In the world of cats, there exists a hierarchy that is as complex and nuanced as any human society. At the top of this feline social ladder are the Alpha cats, the fearless leaders who rule with an iron paw. And then there are the Beta cats, the loyal followers who act as the right-hand cats to the Alphas. These Beta cats may not be in charge, but they play a crucial role in maintaining order within the household.

Claw And Order
Establishing Your Cat's Rank at Home

Chapter 1: The Feline Social Structure

The Beta cats are the unsung heroes of the feline world. They may not get all the attention or glory that the Alphas do, but they are the ones who keep things running smoothly behind the scenes. They are the ones who mediate disputes between other cats, make sure everyone is fed and groomed, and generally keep the peace in the household. In many ways, they are the true power players of the cat world.

But being a Beta cat is not always an easy job. They must constantly navigate the tricky waters of feline politics, making sure to stay on the good side of the Alphas while also keeping the other cats in line. It's a delicate balancing act that requires a mix of diplomacy, cunning, and a healthy dose of catnip.

Claw And Order
Establishing Your Cat's Rank at Home

Chapter 1: The Feline Social Structure

Despite the challenges they face, Beta cats take their role seriously. They understand that without their steady presence and calming influence, the household would descend into chaos. They may not always get the credit they deserve, but they know that their contributions are invaluable in keeping the peace and harmony within the feline community.

So the next time you see your Beta cat quietly going about their business, take a moment to appreciate all that they do. They may not be the ones in the spotlight, but they are the ones who truly make your household a happy and harmonious place for all your furry friends. And remember, behind every great Alpha cat is a loyal Beta cat, ready to lend a paw whenever needed.

Claw And Order
Establishing Your Cat's Rank at Home

Chapter 1: The Feline Social Structure

The Omega Cat: The Underdog or the Master Manipulator?

In the world of feline social hierarchy, there is one cat that often gets overlooked - the Omega Cat. This underdog of the cat world is often seen as the one who doesn't quite fit in with the rest of the pride. But is the Omega Cat truly just a lowly member of the pack, or could they be the master manipulator pulling the strings behind the scenes?

Claw And Order
Establishing Your Cat's Rank at Home

Chapter 1: The Feline Social Structure

Many cat owners may underestimate the Omega Cat, assuming that they are simply the runt of the litter or the cat that always gets picked on by the others. However, don't be fooled by their seemingly meek demeanor. The Omega Cat may actually be the one calling the shots without you even realizing it. They have a way of subtly manipulating the other cats in the household to get what they want, whether it's the best spot on the couch or the last bit of tuna in the bowl.

While the Alpha Cat may be the one who appears to be in charge, it's the Omega Cat who is often the real power player. They know how to use their charm and cunning to get what they want, all while flying under the radar. So next time you think your Omega Cat is just a pushover, think again - they may be the true mastermind of the household.

Claw And Order
Establishing Your Cat's Rank at Home

Chapter 1: The Feline Social Structure

But don't worry, being the Omega Cat doesn't mean they are any less deserving of love and attention. In fact, many cat owners find that their Omega Cat is the most lovable and affectionate of the bunch. They may not be the loudest or most assertive, but they have a way of worming their way into your heart and making you wonder how you ever lived without them.

So, the next time you see your Omega Cat lounging in the sun or snuggled up on your lap, remember that they may just be the unsung hero of the household. They may not be the biggest or the boldest, but they are certainly a force to be reckoned with. Embrace your Omega Cat for the master manipulator that they are, and watch as they continue to win over your heart with their quiet charm and cunning ways.

Claw And Order
Establishing Your Cat's Rank at Home

Chapter 2: Signs Your Cat is Trying to Establish Dominance

The Stare Down: When Fluffy Means Business

Have you ever experienced the intense stare down from your cat that makes you question who is really in charge? Welcome to the world of feline social hierarchy, where Fluffy means business and takes no prisoners. In this subchapter, we will explore the phenomenon of the stare down and how to navigate this tricky territory with your furry overlord.

Claw And Order
Establishing Your Cat's Rank at Home

Chapter 2: Signs Your Cat is Trying to Establish Dominance

When your cat locks eyes with you in a stare down, it's not just a cute moment of bonding - it's a power move. Cats communicate through body language, and the stare down is their way of asserting dominance and establishing their rank within the household. So next time Fluffy gives you the death glare, remember that it's nothing personal - it's just business.

To survive the stare down, it's important to show your cat that you are not to be messed with. Stand your ground, maintain eye contact, and don't back down. This may feel intimidating at first, but remember that you are the human in this relationship and it's up to you to set the boundaries. Show your cat who's boss (even if deep down you know it's really them).

Claw And Order
Establishing Your Cat's Rank at Home

Chapter 2: Signs Your Cat is Trying to Establish Dominance

If the stare down escalates into a full-blown standoff, don't panic. This is just a cat's way of testing your resolve and seeing if you have what it takes to be a worthy member of their social hierarchy. Stay calm, stay strong, and remember that you are the one with the opposable thumbs - a powerful tool in the battle for dominance.

In conclusion, the stare down is a key moment in establishing your cat's rank at home. Embrace the challenge, show your cat that you mean business, and remember that a little humor goes a long way in diffusing tension. With a mix of confidence, respect, and a healthy dose of sarcasm, you can navigate the stare down like a pro and maintain harmony in your feline-dominated household.

Claw And Order
Establishing Your Cat's Rank at Home

Chapter 2: Signs Your Cat is Trying to Establish Dominance

The Tail Twitch: Decoding Feline Body Language

Have you ever wondered what your cat is trying to tell you with that mysterious tail twitch? It turns out, your feline friend's body language is a key indicator of their social hierarchy within your household. In this subchapter, we'll delve into the fascinating world of decoding feline body language, starting with the ever-elusive tail twitch.

**Claw And Order
Establishing Your Cat's Rank at Home**

Chapter 2: Signs Your Cat is Trying to Establish Dominance

When your cat's tail is twitching rapidly, it's a sign that they are feeling agitated or irritated. This could be because they are trying to establish dominance over another cat in the household, or perhaps they are simply annoyed that you haven't fed them yet. Either way, it's important to pay attention to this subtle cue and adjust your behavior accordingly. Remember, in the world of cats, the tail twitch speaks volumes.

Claw And Order
Establishing Your Cat's Rank at Home

Chapter 2: Signs Your Cat is Trying to Establish Dominance

On the other hand, if your cat's tail is held high and twitching gently, it's a sign of contentment and confidence. This is your cat's way of showing that they are comfortable in their role within the household and are happy with their place in the social hierarchy. So next time you see your furry friend strutting around with their tail held high, give them a little extra love and attention – they deserve it for being such a confident kitty!

**Claw And Order
Establishing Your Cat's Rank at Home**

Chapter 2: Signs Your Cat is Trying to Establish Dominance

Of course, not all tail twitches are created equal. If your cat's tail is puffed up like a Halloween decoration, it's a clear sign that they are feeling threatened or scared. This could be because of a loud noise, a new pet in the household, or even just a change in routine. In these situations, it's important to give your cat some space and time to calm down before trying to interact with them. Remember, a puffed-up tail means "back off" in the language of cats.

Claw And Order
Establishing Your Cat's Rank at Home

Chapter 2: Signs Your Cat is Trying to Establish Dominance

In conclusion, understanding your cat's body language, especially the tail twitch, is crucial in deciphering their place in the social hierarchy within your household. By paying attention to these subtle cues and responding accordingly, you can ensure a harmonious and happy relationship with your feline friend. So next time you see that tail twitching, take a moment to decode the message – your cat will thank you for it.

Claw And Order
Establishing Your Cat's Rank at Home

Chapter 2: Signs Your Cat is Trying to Establish Dominance

The Power Play: How Cats Assert Their Authority

Welcome to the wild world of feline power plays! In this subchapter, we'll be diving into the fascinating topic of how cats assert their authority within the household. From subtle body language cues to not-so-subtle demands for treats, our furry friends have a unique way of establishing their rank.

First and foremost, it's important to understand that cats are natural-born leaders. They come from a long line of majestic hunters and rulers of the animal kingdom. So, when your cat struts around the house like they own the place, they're not just being arrogant - they're simply embracing their innate sense of authority.

Claw And Order
Establishing Your Cat's Rank at Home

Chapter 2: Signs Your Cat is Trying to Establish Dominance

One of the most common ways cats assert their dominance is through physical displays of power. This can include things like puffing up their fur to make themselves appear larger, or engaging in playful (but slightly aggressive) wrestling matches with other pets. It's all just part of the game of cat supremacy!

But don't be fooled by their tough exterior - cats also have a softer side when it comes to asserting their authority. They may cuddle up to you for extra attention, or give you the sweetest purrs and headbutts to remind you who's really in charge. It's all part of their cunning plan to keep you under their paw.

**Claw And Order
Establishing Your Cat's Rank at Home**

Chapter 2: Signs Your Cat is Trying to Establish Dominance

So, next time your cat demands to be fed at 3 am or refuses to move from your spot on the couch, just remember that it's all part of their grand scheme to maintain their rank in the household. Embrace the power play, and you'll be well on your way to establishing a harmonious relationship with your furry overlord.

Claw And Order
Establishing Your Cat's Rank at Home

Chapter 3: Strategies for Maintaining Peace in a Multi-Cat Household

Playing Referee: When Cats Clash

As cat owners, we know that living with multiple feline friends can sometimes feel like being the referee in a never-ending wrestling match. Cats are territorial creatures by nature, and when they clash, it can be quite the spectacle. But fear not, dear cat owners, for we are here to help you navigate the choppy waters of feline social hierarchy.

Claw And Order
Establishing Your Cat's Rank at Home

Chapter 3: Strategies for Maintaining Peace in a Multi-Cat Household

When cats clash, it's important to remember that they are simply trying to establish their rank within the household. Just like in the wild, cats have a social hierarchy that they adhere to, and sometimes that means a little roughhousing is in order. But don't worry, most cat fights are just a way for them to work out their differences and establish who's boss.

As the referee in your cat's household, it's important to stay calm and not take sides. Cats are incredibly perceptive creatures, and they can pick up on your emotions. If you get too involved in their scuffle, you may inadvertently make the situation worse. So take a deep breath, grab a catnip toy, and try to distract them from their disagreement.

Claw And Order
Establishing Your Cat's Rank at Home

Chapter 3: Strategies for Maintaining Peace in a Multi-Cat Household

One of the best ways to prevent cat clashes is to provide plenty of resources for your feline friends. This means multiple litter boxes, scratching posts, and feeding stations. Cats are territorial creatures, and if they feel like they have to compete for resources, it can lead to tension and conflict. By providing plenty of resources, you can help minimize the chances of a cat clash breaking out.

Remember, at the end of the day, cats are incredibly social creatures who thrive on companionship. While they may have their disagreements from time to time, it's important to remember that they also have strong bonds with each other. So the next time you find yourself playing referee in a cat clash, just remember that it's all part of the natural order of things. And who knows, maybe you'll even get a good laugh out of their antics.

Claw And Order
Establishing Your Cat's Rank at Home

Chapter 3: Strategies for Maintaining Peace in a Multi-Cat Household

The Importance of Territory: Creating Zones of Control

In the world of cats, territory is everything. Just like humans, cats have a need to establish their own personal space and mark it as their own. Creating zones of control within your home is crucial for maintaining peace and harmony among your feline friends. Whether it's a favorite spot on the couch or a designated scratching post, giving your cat their own territory can help prevent conflicts and keep your household running smoothly.

Claw And Order
Establishing Your Cat's Rank at Home

Chapter 3: Strategies for Maintaining Peace in a Multi-Cat Household

When it comes to establishing zones of control, understanding your cat's social hierarchy is key. Cats are natural born leaders, and they will do whatever it takes to maintain their status within the household. By creating territories for each cat to claim as their own, you can help them feel secure and confident in their position. Just remember, it's important to respect each cat's boundaries and not intrude on their territory without permission. After all, no one likes a nosy neighbor!

Claw And Order
Establishing Your Cat's Rank at Home

Chapter 3: Strategies for Maintaining Peace in a Multi-Cat Household

One of the best ways to create zones of control for your cats is to provide plenty of vertical space. Cats love to climb and perch up high, so investing in a cat tree or shelves can give them the perfect vantage point to survey their domain. Plus, having multiple levels in your home can help prevent territorial disputes by giving each cat their own personal space to relax and unwind. Just make sure to provide plenty of cozy beds and hiding spots to keep everyone happy.

**Claw And Order
Establishing Your Cat's Rank at Home**

Chapter 3: Strategies for Maintaining Peace in a Multi-Cat Household

Another important aspect of creating zones of control is to establish feeding and litter box areas for each cat. Cats are very particular about their food and bathroom habits, so having separate locations for each cat can help prevent conflicts and ensure that everyone gets their fair share. Plus, having designated areas for these essentials can help you monitor your cat's health and behavior more closely. Just be prepared for the occasional turf war over who gets the best sleeping spot near the food bowl!

**Claw And Order
Establishing Your Cat's Rank at Home**

Chapter 3: Strategies for Maintaining Peace in a Multi-Cat Household

In conclusion, establishing zones of control within your home is essential for maintaining peace and order among your feline companions. By understanding your cat's social hierarchy and providing them with plenty of vertical space, designated territories, and separate feeding and litter box areas, you can help prevent conflicts and create a harmonious living environment for all. So go ahead, let your cats stake their claim and watch as they rule the roost with style and grace. After all, in the world of cats, it's all about establishing Claws and Order!

Claw And Order
Establishing Your Cat's Rank at Home

Chapter 3: Strategies for Maintaining Peace in a Multi-Cat Household

Establishing a Hierarchy: The Dos and Don'ts

So, you've brought a new feline friend into your home and now you're wondering how to establish a hierarchy. Don't worry, we've got you covered with some dos and don'ts to help you navigate the tricky world of cat social dynamics.

First things first, do let your cat know who's boss. This doesn't mean being overly aggressive or domineering, but simply setting some boundaries and rules. Cats thrive on structure and routine, so establishing yourself as the leader will help keep the peace in your household.

Claw And Order
Establishing Your Cat's Rank at Home

Chapter 3: Strategies for Maintaining Peace in a Multi-Cat Household

On the flip side, don't let your cat walk all over you. While it's important to be understanding and patient with your furry friend, it's also important to set limits. If your cat starts exhibiting undesirable behavior, like scratching furniture or jumping on countertops, it's important to address it firmly but lovingly.

Another important do is to provide plenty of opportunities for your cat to exercise their natural instincts. Cats are hunters by nature, so make sure to provide plenty of toys and activities that stimulate their senses. A bored cat is a mischievous cat, so keep them entertained and engaged to prevent any unwanted behavior.

Claw And Order
Establishing Your Cat's Rank at Home

Chapter 3: Strategies for Maintaining Peace in a Multi-Cat Household

And finally, don't forget to reward good behavior. Positive reinforcement goes a long way with cats, so be sure to praise and reward your cat when they exhibit desirable behavior. Whether it's a treat, a scratch behind the ears, or a little playtime, showing your cat some love and appreciation will help strengthen your bond and reinforce their place in the hierarchy.

**Claw And Order
Establishing Your Cat's Rank at Home**

Chapter 4: The Role of the Human in the Feline Social Hierarchy

In conclusion, establishing a hierarchy in your household doesn't have to be a daunting task. By following these dos and don'ts, you can create a harmonious environment where both you and your cat can coexist happily. Remember, a little humor and patience go a long way when it comes to understanding your cat's social hierarchy.

Claw And Order
Establishing Your Cat's Rank at Home

Chapter 4: The Role of the Human in the Feline Social Hierarchy

Cat Whisperer or Cat Servant: Finding Your Place

Are you a cat whisperer or just a lowly cat servant in your own home? In this subchapter, we will explore the delicate balance of power in your household and help you find your place in your cat's social hierarchy. It's time to establish some claws and order in your life!

First and foremost, it's important to understand that cats are not just pets - they are rulers of their own little kingdoms. Your fluffy feline friend may seem cute and cuddly, but underneath that adorable exterior lies a cunning and calculating creature who is always plotting their next move. So, embrace your role as a loyal subject to your cat overlord and accept your place in their royal court.

Claw And Order
Establishing Your Cat's Rank at Home

Chapter 4: The Role of the Human in the Feline Social Hierarchy

As a cat owner, it's crucial to recognize the signs of where you stand in your cat's eyes. Are you constantly at their beck and call, catering to their every whim? Congratulations, you are most likely a humble cat servant. On the other hand, if you have mastered the art of interpreting your cat's meows and body language, you may just be a true cat whisperer who understands their needs and desires.

But fear not, dear cat owners, for there is hope for those who find themselves at the bottom of the social ladder in their own homes. By establishing boundaries and asserting your authority, you can slowly climb the ranks and earn the respect of your furry overlord. Remember, it's all about striking the right balance between being a loving companion and a firm leader in your cat's eyes.

**Claw And Order
Establishing Your Cat's Rank at Home**

Chapter 4: The Role of the Human in the Feline Social Hierarchy

So, whether you are a seasoned cat whisperer or a newbie cat servant, remember that establishing claws and order in your household is key to maintaining harmony and balance. Embrace your role as a loyal subject to your feline ruler, and who knows - you may just earn a spot in their royal court as a trusted advisor. Just don't forget to bow down and offer treats to your fluffy overlord on a regular basis!

Claw And Order
Establishing Your Cat's Rank at Home

Chapter 4: The Role of the Human in the Feline Social Hierarchy

Setting Boundaries: When to Step In and When to Let Them Sort It Out

Setting boundaries with your feline friends can be a tricky business. As cat owners, we all want to make sure our fur babies are happy and comfortable in their homes, but sometimes they push the limits a little too far. So, when do we step in and when do we let them sort it out on their own? It's a delicate balance, but with a little humor and a lot of love, we can navigate the wild world of cat social hierarchy together.

**Claw And Order
Establishing Your Cat's Rank at Home**

Chapter 4: The Role of the Human in the Feline Social Hierarchy

First and foremost, it's important to understand that cats are natural-born drama queens. They love to push buttons and test boundaries just to see what they can get away with. So, when your cat is engaging in a little power play with their feline siblings, it's important to know when to step in and when to let them hash it out themselves. If things escalate to the point of hair flying and claws out, it might be time to intervene. But if it's just a little hissing and swatting, it's best to let them sort it out on their own. After all, a little cat fight never hurt anyone (except maybe the pride).

Claw And Order
Establishing Your Cat's Rank at Home

Chapter 4: The Role of the Human in the Feline Social Hierarchy

When it comes to setting boundaries with your cats, consistency is key. If you let Fluffy jump on the kitchen counter one day and then scold her for it the next, she's going to be confused and probably a little annoyed. So, pick your battles and stick to your guns. If you don't want Mittens scratching up the furniture, invest in a good scratching post and redirect her there every time she goes for the couch. And if Mr. Whiskers insists on sleeping on your head at night, well, sometimes you just have to let sleeping cats lie (literally).

Claw And Order
Establishing Your Cat's Rank at Home

Chapter 4: The Role of the Human in the Feline Social Hierarchy

But what about when your cats are fighting over territory or resources? This is where things can get a little hairy (pun intended). It's important to remember that cats are territorial by nature, so conflicts over space or food are bound to happen from time to time. In these situations, it's best to step in and try to diffuse the situation before things get out of hand. Maybe separate the cats for a little while or give them each their own food and water dishes. And if all else fails, just remember that there's always enough love to go around (even if it means buying a second cat tree).

Claw And Order
Establishing Your Cat's Rank at Home

Chapter 4: The Role of the Human in the Feline Social Hierarchy

In the end, setting boundaries with your cats is all about finding a balance between letting them be their wild, independent selves and keeping the peace in your home. So, next time Mittens decides to take a swipe at Fluffy's tail, take a deep breath, pour yourself a glass of wine, and remember that at the end of the day, you're all just a bunch of crazy cat people trying to make it work. And really, what could be more hilarious (and heartwarming) than that?

**Claw And Order
Establishing Your Cat's Rank at Home**

Chapter 4: The Role of the Human in the Feline Social Hierarchy

Cat-Proofing Your Home: Creating a Safe and Harmonious Environment

Welcome to the subchapter on "Cat-Proofing Your Home: Creating a Safe and Harmonious Environment" in our book "Claws and Order: Establishing Your Cat's Rank at Home." As cat owners, we all know that our feline friends can be quite mischievous and curious creatures. In order to maintain peace and order in your household, it's important to take some steps to ensure that your home is cat-proofed.

Claw And Order
Establishing Your Cat's Rank at Home

Chapter 4: The Role of the Human in the Feline Social Hierarchy

First and foremost, it's essential to understand your cat's social hierarchy within the household. Cats are natural hunters and have a strong sense of territory. They will often mark their territory by scratching furniture or spraying urine. To prevent this behavior, provide your cat with plenty of scratching posts and toys to keep them entertained and satisfied.

Another important aspect of cat-proofing your home is making sure that all potential hazards are removed or secured. Cats are known for their curiosity and agility, so be sure to secure any loose cords, toxic plants, and small objects that could be harmful if ingested. Remember, cats have a knack for finding the most obscure places to hide and play, so it's important to be vigilant in keeping your home safe for your furry friend.

**Claw And Order
Establishing Your Cat's Rank at Home**

Chapter 5: The Cats Meow: Communicating Within the Hierarchy

In addition to removing potential hazards, it's also important to create a safe and harmonious environment for your cat. This means providing them with a comfortable and cozy place to rest, plenty of fresh water, and nutritious food. Cats thrive on routine and structure, so be sure to establish a feeding schedule and stick to it.

**Claw And Order
Establishing Your Cat's Rank at Home**

Chapter 5: The Cats Meow: Communicating Within the Hierarchy

Lastly, don't forget to give your cat plenty of love and attention. Cats are social creatures and crave interaction with their humans. Spend time playing with your cat, grooming them, and giving them plenty of affection. By creating a safe and harmonious environment for your cat, you'll ensure that they are happy and content in their home. Remember, a happy cat means a happy owner!

Claw And Order
Establishing Your Cat's Rank at Home

Chapter 5: The Cats Meow: Communicating Within the Hierarchy

Vocalizations: What Your Cat's Sounds Really Mean

Have you ever wondered what your cat is trying to tell you when they meow, purr, or hiss? In this subchapter, we will dive into the world of feline vocalizations and uncover the hidden meanings behind your cat's sounds. Get ready to decode the mysteries of your furry friend's communication skills!

First up, let's talk about meowing. Contrary to popular belief, cats don't meow just to annoy you for a midnight snack. In fact, meowing is their way of communicating with humans, not other cats. So the next time your cat meows incessantly, they might just be trying to tell you they need some attention or affection. Or maybe they're just practicing their opera skills – who knows?

**Claw And Order
Establishing Your Cat's Rank at Home**

Chapter 5: The Cats Meow: Communicating Within the Hierarchy

Next, let's discuss purring. Ah, the soothing sound of a cat purring can be quite relaxing, but what does it really mean? Well, purring is often a sign of contentment and relaxation. Your cat is basically saying, "I'm happy and comfortable right now, so keep the chin scratches coming!" So, if your cat is purring up a storm, you must be doing something right in their eyes.

Now, onto hissing. When your cat hisses, it's a clear sign that they are feeling threatened or scared. It's their way of saying, "Back off, I'm not in the mood for cuddles right now." So, if your cat starts hissing at you, maybe give them some space and approach them later when they're feeling more at ease. Or just invest in some catnip – that usually does the trick!

**Claw And Order
Establishing Your Cat's Rank at Home**

Chapter 5: The Cats Meow: Communicating Within the Hierarchy

In conclusion, understanding your cat's vocalizations can help you navigate their social hierarchy within the household. By paying attention to their meows, purrs, and hisses, you can better communicate with your feline friend and strengthen your bond. So, next time your cat starts meowing non-stop, remember they're just trying to tell you they love you (or they want food – it could go either way). Embrace the quirky world of feline communication and enjoy the endless conversations with your furry companion.

Claw And Order
Establishing Your Cat's Rank at Home

Chapter 5: The Cats Meow: Communicating Within the Hierarchy

The Power of Purring: Comforting or Commanding?

In the world of cats, there is a mysterious power that has fascinated and mystified cat owners for centuries - the power of purring. Is it a comforting gesture from our feline friends, or is it a subtle command to establish their dominance within the household? Let's dive into this purr-fectly intriguing topic in our subchapter titled "The Power of Purring: Comforting or Commanding?"

**Claw And Order
Establishing Your Cat's Rank at Home**

Chapter 5: The Cats Meow: Communicating Within the Hierarchy

First and foremost, let's address the comforting aspect of purring. Cat owners are all too familiar with the soothing sound of their cat's purr as they curl up in their laps or snuggle close during nap time. It's like a gentle massage for the soul, a warm fuzzy blanket of reassurance that everything is right in the world. So, is it possible that our furry friends are simply expressing their love and contentment through their purring? Or are they secretly plotting their next move to assert their dominance?

**Claw And Order
Establishing Your Cat's Rank at Home**

Chapter 5: The Cats Meow: Communicating Within the Hierarchy

On the flip side, some cat behavior experts speculate that purring may actually be a form of subtle manipulation and control. Picture this: your cat purrs loudly as you prepare their dinner, giving off the impression of contentment and gratitude. But in reality, they may be using their purr as a way to command you to serve their meal faster, asserting their dominance as the ruler of the household. Sneaky, right?

**Claw And Order
Establishing Your Cat's Rank at Home**

Chapter 5: The Cats Meow: Communicating Within the Hierarchy

Regardless of whether purring is a comforting gesture or a commanding tactic, one thing is for sure - it's a powerful tool in your cat's arsenal. Understanding the nuances of your cat's purring can help you navigate their social hierarchy within the household and establish your own rank as the ultimate cat whisperer. So, the next time your furry friend starts to purr, listen closely and decode the message they're trying to convey. You just might uncover the secret to maintaining peace and order in your feline kingdom.

Claw And Order
Establishing Your Cat's Rank at Home

Chapter 5: The Cats Meow: Communicating Within the Hierarchy

In conclusion, the power of purring is a fascinating phenomenon that showcases the complex social dynamics of our beloved cats. Whether they're using it to comfort us or command us, one thing is for certain - we are at the mercy of their adorable purring prowess. So, embrace the purr and revel in the joy of being owned by your furry feline overlord. Remember, in the world of cats, purring is not just a sound - it's a language of love, manipulation, and dominance all rolled into one.

Claw And Order
Establishing Your Cat's Rank at Home

Chapter 5: The Cats Meow: Communicating Within the Hierarchy

Body Language: Reading Between the Whiskers

Welcome, cat owners, to the fascinating world of body language! As we all know, cats are masters of communication without saying a word. From the flick of a tail to the twitch of a whisker, our feline friends have a whole language of their own. And today, we're going to focus on one of the most telling indicators of your cat's mood and status within the household: their whiskers.

**Claw And Order
Establishing Your Cat's Rank at Home**

Chapter 5: The Cats Meow: Communicating Within the Hierarchy

If you've ever wondered what your cat is thinking, just take a look at those whiskers. Like a furry antenna, they pick up on all the subtle cues and signals in your cat's environment. Are they relaxed and outstretched? Congratulations, your cat is feeling comfortable and confident. But if those whiskers are pulled back close to their face, watch out - your cat may be feeling anxious or threatened. It's like a mood ring, but on their face!

Claw And Order
Establishing Your Cat's Rank at Home

Chapter 5: The Cats Meow: Communicating Within the Hierarchy

But it's not just about their own feelings - a cat's whiskers can also tell you a lot about their place in the social hierarchy at home. Just like a peacock flaunting its feathers, a cat with outstretched whiskers is showing off their dominance. They're saying, "I'm the boss around here, so watch out!" On the other hand, a cat with their whiskers pulled back may be feeling more submissive, deferring to the alpha cat in the household. It's like a game of Whisker Wars, with each cat vying for the top spot.

Claw And Order
Establishing Your Cat's Rank at Home

Chapter 5: The Cats Meow: Communicating Within the Hierarchy

So, next time you're trying to decipher your cat's behavior, don't forget to pay attention to those whiskers. They may be small, but they pack a big punch when it comes to understanding your cat's social dynamics. And who knows, maybe you'll even pick up a few tricks on how to assert your own dominance at home - just make sure to leave the whisker twitching to the experts. After all, in the world of cats, it's all about reading between the whiskers.

Claw And Order
Establishing Your Cat's Rank at Home

Chapter 6: When the Hierarchy Shifts: Dealing with Changes in Rank

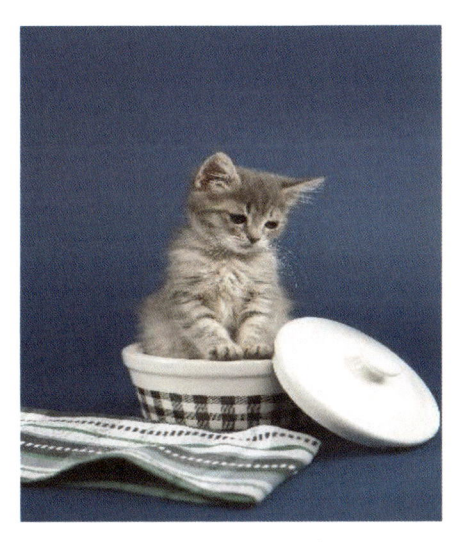

Adding a New Cat to the Mix: Introducing a New Player

So, you've decided to expand your feline family by adding a new cat to the mix. Congratulations! But before you dive headfirst into this new adventure, it's important to understand how to properly introduce your new kitty to the existing members of your fur squad. Think of it as bringing in a new player to your cat's social hierarchy game - it's all about establishing the right pecking order without causing a full-blown cat fight.

**Claw And Order
Establishing Your Cat's Rank at Home**

Chapter 6: When the Hierarchy Shifts: Dealing with Changes in Rank

First things first, make sure to set up a safe space for your new cat to acclimate to their surroundings. Cats are territorial creatures, so it's crucial to give them a separate area where they can feel secure and comfortable. This will also give your existing cats a chance to sniff out the new addition without feeling threatened or territorial.

Next, it's time to start the introductions. Keep in mind that cats are creatures of habit, so it's best to introduce them slowly and gradually. Start by swapping scents between the new and existing cats - this can be done by rubbing a cloth on one cat and then placing it near the other cat. This helps them get familiar with each other's scent before they actually meet face to face.

Claw And Order
Establishing Your Cat's Rank at Home

Chapter 6: When the Hierarchy Shifts: Dealing with Changes in Rank

When the time comes for the big introduction, keep a close eye on their body language. Hissing, growling, and puffed-up tails are all signs of aggression, so be ready to step in and separate them if things get heated. Remember, it's all about establishing a peaceful coexistence within your cat's social hierarchy - no need for any royal cat rumble.

As the days go by, continue to monitor their interactions and provide plenty of positive reinforcement for good behavior. Treats, toys, and extra cuddles can go a long way in helping your cats bond and establish their ranks within the household. And don't forget to give each cat their own space and attention - after all, nobody likes feeling left out in the cat world. With patience, love, and a little bit of humor, you'll have your feline family living in purr-fect harmony in no time.

Claw And Order
Establishing Your Cat's Rank at Home

Chapter 6: When the Hierarchy Shifts: Dealing with Changes in Rank

Dealing with Illness or Aging: Adjusting the Hierarchy

As cat owners, we often find ourselves in a bit of a pickle when our furry friends fall ill or start showing signs of aging. Suddenly, the hierarchy we've established in our homes is thrown out of whack. Fluffy, who used to be the queen bee, is now struggling to keep up with the younger, sprightlier cats in the household. So, how do we adjust the hierarchy to accommodate these changes?

**Claw And Order
Establishing Your Cat's Rank at Home**

Chapter 6: When the Hierarchy Shifts: Dealing with Changes in Rank

First and foremost, it's important to remember that cats are incredibly resilient creatures. They may be feeling a bit under the weather or moving a bit slower than usual, but they are still the same lovable furballs we know and adore. So, when dealing with illness or aging, it's crucial to show them the same love and attention as always, if not more. Let them know they are still a valued member of the household, regardless of their health status.

**Claw And Order
Establishing Your Cat's Rank at Home**

Chapter 6: When the Hierarchy Shifts: Dealing with Changes in Rank

Next, it's time to address the other cats in the household. They may sense that something is different with their feline companion and may try to take advantage of the situation to move up the ranks. It's important to remind them that the hierarchy is still intact, and Fluffy is still the boss. Encourage them to show empathy and support towards their fellow cat, rather than trying to dominate the situation.

As cat owners, we must also be prepared to make some adjustments in our daily routines. This may include providing extra care and attention to the sick or aging cat, ensuring they are comfortable and well-cared for. It may also mean making accommodations for their special needs, such as providing them with easier access to food and water, or creating a cozy spot for them to rest.

**Claw And Order
Establishing Your Cat's Rank at Home**

Chapter 6: When the Hierarchy Shifts: Dealing with Changes in Rank

Finally, don't forget to consult with your vet to ensure your cat is receiving the proper care and treatment. They may have suggestions on how to make your cat more comfortable or may recommend specific medications or therapies to help improve their quality of life. Remember, our cats rely on us to take care of them, especially when they are not feeling their best. By adjusting the hierarchy and providing them with the support they need, we can ensure they live out their golden years in comfort and happiness.

**Claw And Order
Establishing Your Cat's Rank at Home**

Chapter 6: When the Hierarchy Shifts: Dealing with Changes in Rank

Human Interference: When to Step In and When to Let Nature Take Its Course

As cat owners, we often find ourselves caught in the middle of our feline friends' social hierarchy within the household. It can be tempting to intervene when we see a little cat drama unfolding, but sometimes it's best to just sit back and let nature take its course. So, when should you step in and when should you let your cats duke it out on their own? Let's dive in!

**Claw And Order
Establishing Your Cat's Rank at Home**

Chapter 6: When the Hierarchy Shifts: Dealing with Changes in Rank

First and foremost, it's important to remember that cats are highly territorial animals. They have their own ways of establishing rank and sorting out their differences. So, if you see your cats engaging in a little scuffle over who gets the best spot on the couch, don't be too quick to break it up. They're just trying to sort out their hierarchy, and it's all part of the natural order of things.

However, there are times when human interference is necessary. If you see one of your cats consistently bullying another, it's time to step in and put a stop to it. Nobody likes a bully, not even in the feline world. So, don't be afraid to assert your authority and make it clear that such behavior will not be tolerated in your household.

**Claw And Order
Establishing Your Cat's Rank at Home**

Chapter 6: When the Hierarchy Shifts: Dealing with Changes in Rank

On the flip side, there are also times when it's best to let nature take its course. For example, if your cats are playfully wrestling with each other, there's no need to intervene unless things start to get too rough. Cats have a way of working things out on their own, and sometimes a little roughhousing is just their way of bonding and establishing their place in the hierarchy.

In the end, finding the right balance between stepping in and letting nature take its course is key to maintaining a harmonious household with multiple cats. So, trust your instincts, observe your cats' behavior closely, and remember that a little cat drama is all part of the fun of being a cat owner. Embrace the chaos, and your feline friends will thank you for it in their own purr-fect way!

Claw And Order
Establishing Your Cat's Rank at Home

Chapter 7: The Ultimate Guide to Keeping the Peace Among Feline Roommates

The Importance of Routine: Setting Expectations Early

In the world of cats, routine is key to maintaining peace and order within your feline family. Setting expectations early on is crucial to establishing your cat's rank at home. Without a clear routine, chaos can ensue, and your cat may start to believe they are the ruler of the house (which, let's be honest, they probably already think they are).

Claw And Order -Establishing Your Cat's Rank at Home

Claw And Order
Establishing Your Cat's Rank at Home

Chapter 7: The Ultimate Guide to Keeping the Peace Among Feline Roommates

Imagine a world where your cat dictates when they are fed, when they are played with, and when they are allowed on the furniture. Sounds like a nightmare, right? By setting a routine and sticking to it, you are showing your cat that you are the boss (even if they still refuse to acknowledge it).

Cats thrive on routine because it provides them with a sense of security and predictability. When they know what to expect, they are less likely to act out or become anxious. Plus, routines can help prevent behavioral issues such as aggression or excessive meowing. So, by establishing a routine early on, you are not only setting expectations for your cat, but also creating a harmonious environment for everyone in the household.

**Claw And Order
Establishing Your Cat's Rank at Home**

Chapter 7: The Ultimate Guide to Keeping the Peace Among Feline Roommates

But don't worry, setting a routine doesn't mean you have to become a strict disciplinarian. In fact, routines can be fun for both you and your cat. For example, make meal times a bonding experience by incorporating playtime or training sessions before feeding. This not only helps establish a routine, but also strengthens the bond between you and your furry friend. And let's be honest, who doesn't love a well-fed, well-behaved cat?

**Claw And Order
Establishing Your Cat's Rank at Home**

Chapter 7: The Ultimate Guide to Keeping the Peace Among Feline Roommates

So, cat owners, remember the importance of routine when it comes to setting expectations early with your feline friends. By establishing a routine, you are not only creating a sense of order within your cat's social hierarchy, but also ensuring a happy and harmonious home for everyone. And who knows, maybe one day your cat will finally admit that you are the true ruler of the household (but let's not hold our breath).

Claw And Order
Establishing Your Cat's Rank at Home

Chapter 7: The Ultimate Guide to Keeping the Peace Among Feline Roommates

The Power of Play: Strengthening Bonds and Establishing Order

Welcome to the subchapter on "The Power of Play: Strengthening Bonds and Establishing Order" in our book, "Claws and Order: Establishing Your Cat's Rank at Home." As cat owners, we know that our feline friends have their own unique social hierarchy within the household. And what better way to navigate this hierarchy than through the power of play?

Claw And Order -Establishing Your Cat's Rank at Home

**Claw And Order
Establishing Your Cat's Rank at Home**

Chapter 7: The Ultimate Guide to Keeping the Peace Among Feline Roommates

Playtime isn't just about having fun - it's also a crucial tool for strengthening bonds between cats and their humans. By engaging in interactive play sessions with your cat, you are not only providing them with much-needed mental and physical stimulation, but you are also building trust and establishing your role as the alpha cat in the household. So grab a wand toy or a laser pointer and get ready to strengthen those bonds!

> **Claw And Order
> Establishing Your Cat's Rank at Home**

Chapter 7: The Ultimate Guide to Keeping the Peace Among Feline Roommates

But playtime isn't just about bonding - it's also a way to establish order within the household. Cats are natural hunters, and playtime allows them to satisfy their predatory instincts in a safe and controlled environment. By engaging in regular play sessions with your cat, you are giving them an outlet for their energy and helping to prevent destructive behaviors such as scratching or aggression. Plus, it's a great way to establish boundaries and reinforce your position as the leader of the pack (or should I say, pride?).

**Claw And Order
Establishing Your Cat's Rank at Home**

Chapter 7: The Ultimate Guide to Keeping the Peace Among Feline Roommates

So the next time your cat pounces on a toy mouse or chases after a feather wand, remember that they are not just playing - they are also strengthening their bonds with you and establishing order within the household. Embrace the power of play and watch as your cat's behavior improves and your relationship grows stronger. After all, a household that plays together, stays together!

In conclusion, play is a powerful tool for cat owners to strengthen bonds with their feline companions and establish order within the household. By engaging in regular play sessions, you are not only providing your cat with essential mental and physical stimulation, but you are also reinforcing your role as the alpha cat in the household. So grab a toy, get ready to pounce, and let the games begin! Remember, a happy cat is a well-played cat.

Claw And Order
Establishing Your Cat's Rank at Home

Chapter 7: The Ultimate Guide to Keeping the Peace Among Feline Roommates

Love and Attention: The Key to a Happy and Harmonious Feline Hierarchy

Welcome, cat owners, to the purr-fect guide for understanding your cat's social hierarchy within the household. In this subchapter, we will delve into the importance of love and attention in maintaining a peaceful and harmonious feline kingdom.

First and foremost, let's address the fact that cats are not just cute furry creatures that roam around the house. They are sophisticated beings with their own social structure and rules. Understanding and respecting this hierarchy is crucial for a happy home environment.

**Claw And Order
Establishing Your Cat's Rank at Home**

Chapter 7: The Ultimate Guide to Keeping the Peace Among Feline Roommates

Now, you may be wondering, how can love and attention play a role in establishing your cat's rank at home? Well, just like humans, cats crave affection and companionship. By showering your feline friend with love and attention, you are not only strengthening your bond but also showing them that they are valued members of the family.

In a household with multiple cats, it's important to ensure that each feline receives equal amounts of love and attention. This will help prevent jealousy and competition, ultimately leading to a more peaceful coexistence. Remember, a happy cat is a cat that feels loved and appreciated.

**Claw And Order
Establishing Your Cat's Rank at Home**

Chapter 7: The Ultimate Guide to Keeping the Peace Among Feline Roommates

So, cat owners, remember to prioritize love and attention in your feline hierarchy. By doing so, you are not only creating a harmonious environment for your cats but also strengthening your bond with them. After all, a happy cat means a happy home.

Claw And Order
Establishing Your Cat's Rank at Home

Chapter 8: Conclusion: Embracing the Feline Hierarchy

The Joy of Cat-archy: Finding the Humor and Beauty in Feline Social Dynamics

Are you a proud cat owner who is constantly amused by the quirky social dynamics of your feline friends? If so, welcome to the club! In this subchapter, we will explore the joy of cat-archy and how to find humor and beauty in the sometimes chaotic world of feline social hierarchy within your household.

Claw And Order -Establishing Your Cat's Rank at Home

Claw And Order
Establishing Your Cat's Rank at Home

Chapter 8: Conclusion: Embracing the Feline Hierarchy

One of the most entertaining aspects of living with cats is watching them establish their rank within the home. From the regal king of the castle to the mischievous troublemaker who always seems to be one step ahead, each cat brings a unique personality to the social mix. It's like living in a real-life soap opera, complete with drama, comedy, and plenty of unexpected plot twists.

But let's not forget the beauty of feline social dynamics as well. Cats have a way of forming strong bonds with their fellow feline housemates, often engaging in playful antics and affectionate grooming sessions that warm the heart. It's a reminder that even in the midst of power struggles and territory disputes, there is always room for love and friendship among our furry companions.

**Claw And Order
Establishing Your Cat's Rank at Home**

Chapter 8: Conclusion: Embracing the Feline Hierarchy

As cat owners, it's important to understand and respect the social hierarchy that naturally emerges among our pets. By observing their behavior and body language, we can gain valuable insights into their relationships and help foster a harmonious living environment for all. Plus, it's just plain fun to sit back and watch the show unfold, like a never-ending sitcom starring our favorite feline characters.

So next time you catch your cats engaging in a heated stare-down over a favorite sleeping spot or playfully chasing each other through the house, take a moment to appreciate the joy of cat-archy. Embrace the humor and beauty of their social dynamics, and remember that while cats may rule the roost, we are the lucky ones who get to share our homes with these fascinating creatures. After all, who needs reality TV when you have a house full of cats?

Claw And Order
Establishing Your Cat's Rank at Home

Chapter 8: Conclusion: Embracing the Feline Hierarchy

Your Cat's Rank at Home: Embracing the Quirks and Personalities of Your Feline Family

Have you ever wondered where your cat stands in the social hierarchy of your household? It may surprise you to learn that your feline friend may be more of a boss than you think! Cats have their own unique personalities and quirks that dictate their rank at home, and it's important to embrace and understand these traits to maintain a harmonious relationship with your furry family member.

**Claw And Order
Establishing Your Cat's Rank at Home**

Chapter 8: Conclusion: Embracing the Feline Hierarchy

First and foremost, it's essential to recognize that cats are natural born leaders. They may not be the ones paying the bills or doing the grocery shopping, but in their minds, they are the rulers of the roost. From their regal posture to their demanding meows, cats exude an air of authority that is hard to ignore. So next time your cat gives you that "feed me now" look, remember who's really in charge!

Chapter 8: Conclusion: Embracing the Feline Hierarchy

Each cat has its own unique personality that shapes its rank within the household. Some cats are social butterflies, constantly seeking attention and affection from their human companions. These cats may be more likely to assert themselves as top cat, demanding the best napping spots and first dibs on treats. On the other hand, more introverted cats may prefer to quietly observe from the sidelines, content to let their more outgoing counterparts take the lead.

Claw And Order
Establishing Your Cat's Rank at Home

Chapter 8: Conclusion: Embracing the Feline Hierarchy

It's important to remember that just like people, cats have their own individual preferences and boundaries. Some cats may be perfectly content to share their space with other pets, while others may prefer to be the sole ruler of the household. By understanding and respecting your cat's unique personality, you can help create a peaceful and harmonious living environment for both you and your feline family members.

Chapter 8: Conclusion: Embracing the Feline Hierarchy

In the grand scheme of things, your cat's rank at home may seem like a trivial matter. But to your furry friend, it's a matter of pride and prestige. By embracing and celebrating your cat's quirks and personalities, you can strengthen the bond between you and your feline family members, creating a happy and harmonious home for all. So next time your cat struts around like they own the place, just remember – they probably do!

**Claw And Order
Establishing Your Cat's Rank at Home**

Chapter 8: Conclusion: Embracing the Feline Hierarchy

The Claws and Order Way: Establishing Harmony and Balance in Your Multi-Cat Household

Welcome to the Claws and Order Way, where we strive to establish harmony and balance in your multi-cat household. As any cat owner knows, managing a group of feline furballs can be a tricky task. But fear not, with a little understanding of your cat's social hierarchy, you can create a peaceful coexistence among your beloved pets.

First and foremost, it's important to recognize that cats are natural-born rulers. They have a keen sense of hierarchy and will establish their own pecking order within your household. This means that you may have one cat who reigns supreme, while others fall in line accordingly. It's all about finding that delicate balance of power and respect among your furry companions.

Claw And Order
Establishing Your Cat's Rank at Home

Chapter 8: Conclusion: Embracing the Feline Hierarchy

To maintain peace in your multi-cat household, it's crucial to establish rules and boundaries early on. Cats thrive on routine and structure, so setting clear expectations for behavior will help prevent any power struggles or conflicts. Whether it's designated feeding times, separate sleeping areas, or designated play spaces, creating a structured environment will help your cats understand their place in the hierarchy.

In addition to setting boundaries, it's important to provide plenty of resources for your cats to avoid any territorial disputes. This means having multiple litter boxes, scratching posts, and feeding stations to prevent any competition for resources. Cats are creatures of habit, so ensuring that each cat has their own space and resources will help maintain harmony in your household.

**Claw And Order
Establishing Your Cat's Rank at Home**

Chapter 8: Conclusion: Embracing the Feline Hierarchy

Remember, a little humor goes a long way when managing a multi-cat household. Embrace the chaos and quirks of your feline friends, and don't be afraid to laugh at the absurdity of their antics. By understanding your cat's social hierarchy and embracing the Claws and Order Way, you can create a peaceful and balanced environment for all of your furry companions to thrive.

Printed in Great Britain
by Amazon